TYRANNY OF WORDS

Manipulation of The Mind, The Media, and The Masses

Treval Manne

Very Good Book Publisher

Contents

INTRODUCTION

The goal of this book is to introduce you to the concept of manipulation at a personal level, a societal level, and to explore the implications of manipulation on Mental, Physical, Moral, Economic, and Political spheres. As we review the literature together, consider the times when you have been manipulated, and the times that you have manipulated others.

CHAPTER 1: MANIPULATION IN YOUR RELATIONSHIPS

When discussing the topic of manipulation, it is important to begin with the most fundamental Manipulation, which takes place between two individuals. Stritrof discusses the definitions of manipulation and the effects it can have on your partner, you child, and your parents.

"People who manipulate use mental twisting and emotional exploitation to influence and control others. They intend to have power and control over others to get what they want.

Someone who manipulates you knows your weaknesses and will use them against you. It will continue to happen except if you effectively and certainly stop it. That said, it is not always a piece of cake.

Stopping manipulation in a relationship can be difficult because it might have started subtly. Over time, manipulative behavior in relationships can become the everyday dynamic with your partner."[i]

What Is Manipulation?

Stritof continues to define the motives and techniques of manipulators.

"Manipulation is a tactic someone uses to gain control over another person, usually to get what they want, and often at the other person's expense.

For instance, a manipulative person might use strategies like lying, gaslighting, being passive-aggressive, giving you the silent treatment, among others, all to get you to believe that you are wrong and they are right."[ii]

How do children manipulate their parents?

Early home life can set a precedent for how a person will grow to manipulate or be manipulated by others and is therefore important to understand. Stritof continues,

"Kids manipulate their parents. It's part of their routine. They figure out how to utilize their charms and assets to get everything they might want and negotiate more power in the family.

From one perspective, a few terms of manipulation by kids are innocuous. For example, if your daughter needs to go to a dance on a Saturday night, she's extra charming to you that week. Still, at the same time, she's getting good grades, trustworthy, and doing her chores, so she ought to have the option to go. The display of appeal is sweet, appropriate, and innocuous."[iii]

When a Child's Manipulative Behavior Is a Problem

"In this kind of manipulation, the kid tells you, "Give me my way or face my poo." at the end of the day, "If I don't get everything I might want, I will raise hell for you." In the present circumstance, the control turns into a power and control game for the youngster, and that is the place where it gets risky for guardians.

At the point when children grapple with their folks for power and command over things, the kid does nasty things, and the guardians do useless things. The kid talks oppressively or throws a tantrum, which is an incorrect method for getting what he needs."[iv]

The beginnings of a reliance on manipulation to achieve one's goals can be seen early on. Watch for the signs in your own children if you have them.

Responding to the Power Thrust

"Whenever a youngster utilizes a power push to get everything he might want, you should be extremely cautious about how you answer. you can't yield, and you can't haggle while the child is in that perspective. Assuming that your kid raises his voice at you when he hears the word no or shouts at you, say this:

"We won't discuss this assuming that you speak loudly or, on the other hand, assuming you begin to undermine me."
Assuming a child protests and gets a little loudmouthed while heading to his room or en route to do a task, that is not a powerful thrust. I'm talking about intimidating, threatening behavior. This is manipulation that is intended to make you back down.
When kids use this type of behavior, they've acted out in the past and have gotten their way. Most parents know what's coming. So when you see it coming, remember: the discussion about whether he can go to the dance with his friends is over. The debate is, "You have to manage your voice and behavior.""[vi]

Splitting the Parents

"Another form of manipulation children use is to split their parents. They'll go to the parent they think is the weakest link or the one who has wavered in the past to gain power. Suppose both parents agree that homework has to be done for the entire week before the kid's weekend starts. In that case, the teacher says that the child's assignments aren't done from Tuesday to Friday night. The child can't start watching TV, playing video games, or going out until that homework's done.
As parents, you both have to decide the plan and follow it. There can be no good reasons, whether the kid is, as a rule, adorable to escape doing schoolwork or whether he pitches a fit to receive in return. The two strategies are manipulative, and they ought to be managed similarly."[vii]

Two Parents, One Plan

"Suppose you have a manipulative child, and you decide on specific strategies to manage that manipulative behavior. In that case, both parents have to be on the same page with their values and plan. Both need to agree and have the option to tell the kid:
If you forget to carry your books home, you either borrow a book from a companion and finish the work, or you don't get to go out until the following end of the week."

Try not to set up a circumstance where the father or mother surrenders and lets the kid free if they cry, whimper, argue, oppose, carry on, or lay on the appeal. Stay on course.

Kids watch their folks professionally. It's their work. It's their main thing. Also, they realize their folks have more power than they do. So they advance rapidly, which parent can be controlled and the amount it will take to get that parent to surrender. A few guardians will give in when the kid applies more appeal and warmth. Different guardians give in when the youngster blows up, shouts, and gets oppressive.

It would help if you rested assured your youngster knows the stuff to make you back down. So it might be ideal assuming that you made sure to discuss your arrangement for dealing with this way of behaving as guardians and remain in total agreement. Never say, "I'll converse with Dad about it," on the off chance that you disagree with something Dad has chosen. Never do that.

It's the youngster's liability to resolve it with the guardians correctly. Whenever guardians deviate, they need to deal with it secretly. Assuming the outcomes change, they ought to be changed by the parent who designated them, so the guardians stay enabled."[viii]

How to Cope With Manipulative Family Members

The adult members of your family might decide to be manipulative as well. When such situations occur, we can turn to Ruby Oliver for a straightforward process that describes what to do:

"Follow these 5 steps to learn how to deal with manipulative family members.

1. Find out which family members are victims of the manipulator's tactics. Then communicate your concerns with them as a group.

2. Contemplate what is happening inside of your mind. What intrinsic pieces of yourself have become involuntary reactions to the manipulator? Do you think what you want to believe or what someone else wants you to believe?

3. Set boundaries with the manipulator. Once you have contemplated what is actually you and what the manipulator wants you to think is you, identify the boundaries between you and the person manipulating you. Then verbally and non-verbally set boundaries. Focus on preventing the person from influencing your thoughts, feelings, and actions.

4. Choose the environment in which you engage the manipulator. The person who wants you to control them does it in a place that will make the end goal easier. They want you to be surrounded by others who will back them up, even if unknowingly. Choose a natural location when you are ready to set verbal boundaries.

5. Have patience, and be the bigger person. A manipulator relies on patterns. Breaking these patterns takes time and effort. Be forgiving, and allow the manipulator time and space to change habits. It is their choice,

though, so if they choose not to stop controlling others, then have patience and understanding for yourself and the decision you will have to make.

The sad truth is that many families experience the splintered effect at the hands of the scheming member. Walking away from your family is the last resort, even though sometimes necessary. Up until that point, it's imperative to use every tool in your social skills toolbox. You aren't likely to get the dishonest person to change, but you may be able to set clear boundaries that they can not cross.

In the end, we care about them. They are family, and even if they play the kind of games most call drama, we still love them. That only resolves our center find a way to learn help turn a manipulative relationship into a functional one."[ix]

How to Tell If Someone Is Manipulating You—And What to Do About It

Shortsleeve from Time magazine has advice for those of you who may be wondering whether or not they are in a manipulative relationship with one or more people in your life. Identifying the situation appropriately and responding in the right way are important.

"It could be manipulation if you've ever felt like something is off in a close relationship or casual encounter—you're being pressured, controlled, or even feel like you're questioning yourself more than usual.

There are many different forms of manipulation, ranging from a pushy salesperson to an emotionally abusive partner—and some behaviors are more accessible to spot than others.

Here, experts explain the telltale signs that you could be the subject of manipulation."

You feel fear, obligation, and guilt.

"According to Stines, manipulative behavior involves fear, obligation, and guilt. "When someone is manipulating you, you are being psychologically coerced into doing something you probably don't want to do," she says. You might feel scared to do it, obligated to do it, or guilty about not doing it.

She points to two standard manipulators: "the bully" and "the victim." She says, "a bully makes you feel fearful and might use aggression, threats, and intimidation to control you. The victim engenders a feeling of guilt in their target. "The victim usually acts hurt," Stine says. But while manipulators often play the victim, the reality is that they are the ones who have caused the problem, she adds.

A person targeted by manipulators who play the victim often tries to help the manipulator stop feeling guilty, Stines says. Targets of this kind of manipulation often feel responsible for assisting the victim by doing whatever they can to stop their suffering."

You're questioning yourself.

"The term "gaslighting" is often used to identify manipulation that gets people to question themselves, their reality, memory, or thoughts. A manipulative person might twist what you say and make it about them, hijack the conversation, or make you feel like you've done something wrong when you're not quite sure you have.

If you're being gaslighted, you might feel a false sense of guilt or defensiveness—like you failed ultimately or must have done something wrong when, in reality, that's not the case.

"Manipulators blame," she says. "They don't take responsibility."[x]

There are strings attached.

""If a favor is not done for you just because it isn't 'for fun and free,'" says Stines. "If there are strings attached, then manipulation is occurring."

Stines refers to one type of manipulator as 'Mr. Nice Guy.' This person might be helpful and do a lot of favors for other people. "It is very confusing because you don't realize anything negative is going on," she says. "But, on the other hand, with every good deed, there is a string attached—an expectation." If you don't meet the manipulator's expectations, you will be made out to be ungrateful.

Exploiting the norms and expectations of reciprocity is one of the most common forms of manipulation."

Manipulation is not new, and the common tactics are easy to spot when you know where to look.

"Often, manipulators try one of two tactics. The first is the foot-in-the-door technique, in which someone starts with a small and reasonable request—like, *do you have the time?*—which then leads to a more significant request—like *I need $10 for a taxi.* "This is commonly used in street scams," Olson says."

"The door-in-the-face technique is the opposite—it involves someone making a big request, having it rejected, then creating a smaller one, Olson explains.
Someone doing contract work, for example, may ask you for a large sum of money upfront, and then after you decline, will ask for a smaller amount, he says. This works because, following the more significant request, the minor appeal seems reasonable comparatively, Olson says."[xi]

What to do if you think you're being manipulated

Now that you or a loved one know that you are being manipulated, the path forward is dependent on the specifics of the situation.

"How you react to manipulation depends mainly on what kind of manipulation you face.
Suppose you think you or someone you know is in a manipula-

tive or abusive relationship. In that case, A good support group can help, too, says Stines. "People in toxic relationships need to hear counterpoints somewhere. They are conditioned to think the interactions are normal. Someone needs to help them break out of that assumption."

"Stines suggests trying not to allow the manipulative behavior to affect you personally for other forms of manipulation. "Use the motto, 'Observe don't absorb,'" she notes. After all: "We aren't responsible for anyone else's feelings."
Often, establishing boundaries can play an essential role in keeping manipulation at bay. "People who manipulate have lousy boundaries," Stines says. "You have your own voluntary experience as a human being. You need to know where you end, and the other person begins. Manipulators often have either boundaries that are too rigid or enmeshed."

"In a manipulative situation, it can also help to delay your response. For example, refrain from signing a contract at first glance, don't make a large purchase without thinking it through, and avoid making major relationship decisions the first time they're brought up, he suggests. "'Sleeping on it'" is often the best solution to avoid being manipulated."[xii]

Manipulation at a personal level is bound to happen to each of us. Even more so is the mass manipulation of millions of people at a time. In the Next Chapter, we will discuss how mass manipulators get what they want through advertising, cultural media, and other techniques.

CHAPTER 2: HOW MEDIA IS USED TO MANIPULATE SOCIETY

Media Manipulation in Mass Society

One of the primary methods by which the masses are manipulated is by the media they consume. The desire of companies, Governments, and powerful individuals to make people behave or believe certain ways is made apparent by their advertising, marketing, and manipulative techniques.

Abrozy and Sokolovska discuss the matter of advertising's effect on society and the individual at length.

Direct Marketing and Advertising

"With the rise of marketing in the 1950s, people thought that advertising couldn't affect their habits and the way they choose products. The offered products are described correctly with informative details. Everybody knows that they exist and can have it for some price. Man is creating advertising with complex psychological means that obstruct the cognitive sphere. Advertising is a presentation of products in every form to put them on the market But where is advertising from the field of culture and art? Where is the ad about ethical topics?

Where is advertising from science and research? The emotional content of the message is focused on the necessary feelings, ac-

tivating members of the group, addressing their desires and motives. Properly targeted advertising can create a history for the products - the benefits are sideways.
Advertising is not just about promoting products and services but also promoting a particular way of life and lifestyle."[xiii]

Subconscious Advertising and Cultural Alteration

Abrozy and Sokolovska continue to describe how advertisers use not only direct advertisement, but also subconscious manipulation, to implant the concept of consumption into the mind of the masses.

"A very sophisticated advertising psychology tool is acting at the level of subconsciousness and appealing directly to the fundamental, essential instincts and the destinies of the recipient. Advertising and psychology is a necessary tool for implementing such tools to influence the recipient to uncritically perceive a mass culture that suppresses many traditional standards of behavior that man has gained centuries of experience and overthrow the system of values and motivates the recipient to the desired effect of accepting consumer capitalism, values that are determined by the goal of occupying markets, pillaging resources, and the accumulation of capital available to owners of production resources. The primary purpose of marketing companies and their affiliated media companies is to create a consumer generation dependent on the cheap way of entertainment. Properly targeted advertising can generate history for the products - the benefits are sideways."[xiv]

Watch Time Over Quality

In many ways, the situation described by Ambrozy and Sokolovska has manifested in the world of Television, and also in the online world, where advertisements are directed and calculated to reach the eyes of viewers who log in everyday to watch videos, read articles, and scroll on social media platforms.

"Best is not the media product with the highest quality, but the most-watched one because the view is equal to profit. Advertising plays a significant role in the mass media world. Because it is not always ethical, man must be careful. Man becomes addicted to emotional stimuli and seeks constant satisfaction. The merit of human happiness has become material and satisfying pleasures."

Entertainment as Identity

The pleasures that are felt while viewing and consuming media and culture can develop a person into a new identity.

"Entertainment is a component of a modern leisure culture tasked with destroying free time. Entertainment allows you to move around the world that you can see on TV. What is offered as entertainment does not determine anyone. Still, there is a sufficient basis for work on one's own "identity."

The Human Problem

An identity built on popular television, products, services, and concepts of media might seem like a harmless part of our modern era, but the problem goes deeper.

"Forms and levels of entertainment, mass culture, or, more precisely, "culture for the masses" are undoubtedly the main problem of contemporary culture, which become a culture of enjoyment or a "culture of entertainment." It influences social consciousness much more than it used to be. In particular, the mass media determine models of mass culture and entertainment, the effect of which is to "brainwash ." The media boulevard, literally terrorizing people's thinking, offering disgust, jumbling with half-truths and lies, infects man with moral schizophrenia. Why is the boulevard doing so? Unfortunately, it is mostly in us people. Man is a biological creature, has a tendency to enjoy the misfortune of others, he uses himself in gossip, in sexual excesses, he likes to look at brutality and violence."

While a man in himself might have sexual urges or brutal fantasies, a man can be self-controlled and not feed into such urges, however, with an identity that is mired in the popular media of the masses, such self-constraint is denormalized.

Current advances in media bring people closer to content than before possible. The use of Augmented and virtual reality can satisfy consumers and keep them jumbled in the aforementioned half-truths and lies.

How the Media Manipulates You Without Your Knowing

Now that we have identified the overall results and motivations behind the media and advertising, let us review specific techniques used to manipulate the masses. While the previous section focused on the marketing motives for media manipulation, the next article discusses the manipulative techniques that can be employed for political and economic gain.

Distraction

"The strategy of distraction consists of deviating the public's attention from important issues. They do it by flooding the news with stories on trivial matters. The objective is to distract the people and keep their minds occupied. The result is that people stop questioning why the media isn't talking about specific issues; the people forget the real problems.[xv]

Problem – Reaction – Solution

This method is the equivalent of doing a "poll "in politics. It consists of testing the population by spreading rumors or ideas to evaluate how the people would receive them. It is creating a problem to solve later. Then the public sees the manipulators as heroes.

Gradualism

Gradualism manipulates the people by getting them to accept socially unjust decisions. The key is to do it progressively, slowly, over the years.

For example, say the objective is to fire 80% of the staff of a large, high-profile company. The media would begin to incorporate negative news about the company: sales drops, stock market crashes, rumors, etc. Slowly, it would create awareness and start preparing people for the "big news. "If the layoffs had been made known initially, there would have been a public uproar.

Differing

Another strategy Timsit includes in media manipulation is that of presenting unpopular decisions as *"necessary," "for a better future,"* or *"for our good."* They make the public genuinely believe that their sacrifices will significantly improve things later.

So the citizens get used to a lower quality of life. They start seeing it as usual. Ultimately, the people will resign themselves to the current state of things and stop demanding what they were demanding.

Treating the people like children

The more the media wants to manipulate the public, the more they will talk to the public like they're children. Sugarcoated arguments, characters, and intonations are used as if the people were too weak or immature to handle the truth. The goal is also a submissive, docile reaction. The idea is to keep people from thinking critically like adults.

Appealing to emotions

Emotional appeals are much more potent than sterile, purely objective ones. The media knows it, so they appeal to the public's emotions. Again, they try to keep people from thinking critically and control their thoughts. Remember how powerful fear can be.

Keeping the public ignorant and mediocre

According to Timsit, the media prefers an ignorant, uncultured public. Keeping them isolated from knowledge makes them easier to manipulate. It also keeps insubordination and rebellion away. *Information is power.*

Encouraging people to contribute to mediocrity

This point and the previous one are very similar. This one is one of the most subtle media manipulation strategies. Do the shows offered on TV match what the general public wants? Or are they imposed on us by the media? In other words, *do we watch what we want to watch or what they want us to watch?*

For Timsit, the answer is clear. Consumerism and banality are hypnotizing us. Therefore, we don't care about our surroundings, having been trained to be mediocre.

Self-blame

At the same time that the media encourages our ignorance, they also make us believe that we're the only ones responsible for our misfortunes. The media tells us that our scarce skills will make us miserable and unsuccessful. They seek self-incrimination through self-exculpation and keep the public from mobilizing."[xvi]

The next time you notice one of the techniques being used, point it out and ask, "Why am I being told this in this way? Who does this benefit." Much of the time, the answer is not you.

CHAPTER 3: IS MANIPULATION BAD?

There are tangible consequences to receiving or performing manipulation on others. The mental, physical, and moral issues are discussed in this chapter

Mental Health of Manipulators

In Chapter 1, we briefly discussed the ways in which manipulators get what they want. Sometimes, manipulators may feel that there is no other way to get what they want or that they are powerless to stop their manipulative behaviors. GoodTherapy discusses some of the underlying issues that cause manipulative people to manifest.

"While most people engage in manipulation occasionally, a chronic pattern of manipulation can indicate an underlying mental health concern.

Manipulation is widespread with personality disorder diagnoses such as borderline personality (BPD) and narcissistic personality (NPD). For many with BPD, manipulation may be a means of meeting their emotional needs or obtaining validation. It often occurs when the person with BPD feels insecure or abandoned. As many people with BPD have witnessed or experienced abuse, manipulation may have developed as a coping mechanism to get needs met indirectly.

Individuals with narcissistic personalities (NPD) may have different reasons for engaging in manipulative behavior. As those with

NPD may have difficulty forming close relationships, they may resort to manipulation to "keep" their partner in the relationship. Characteristics of narcissistic manipulation may include shaming, blaming, playing the "victim," control issues, and gaslighting."[xvii]

If you find yourself indulging in too much manipulation, and you are affecting the people around you, consider seeking out a professional counselor to work through the underlying traumas and motivations that may be fueling the behavior.

5 Long-Term Effects of Manipulation

If you are on the receiving end of manipulation for too long, consider the following long term effects from OptimistMinds.

1. Trust Issues

"You have deep-seated trust issues.
Is it hard for you to accept compliments or favors from others? Do you assume that they might have some hidden motives?
Being excessively wary about people's intentions and feeling protective all the time are natural consequences of chronic manipulation. More often than not, the people who emotionally abuse you are the ones you expect love and care from.
When these people breach your trust and take advantage of you, it's scary to be vulnerable again. It becomes hard to accept affection later, even if it's coming from a natural source. The hesitance holds you back in life as trust is a prerequisite to meaningful relationships."[xviii]

2. Poor Boundaries

"You struggle with boundaries.
Would you call yourself a people pleaser? Do you find it hard to say no when you don't want something?
Emotional abuse and manipulation can warp a person's sense of boundaries. As a result, your borders may be porous, not very clear, or rigid, where they're inflexible.
In some cases, you cannot speak up when someone says or does

things that hurt or inconvenience you.

You might have your guard up at other times, not willing to make any exceptions, even if it will be good for you.

Healthy boundaries allow us to be assertive or flexible when needed to stay at peace and not hold ourselves back. But unfortunately, we lose our ability to establish them when the trust issues from manipulation clash with our natural need for love and care."[xix]

3.Emotional Outbursts

"It impacts how your brain works.

Are you prone to emotional outbursts? Do you find it hard to process your feelings and express them healthy ways?

Manipulation can lead to long-term emotional scars that affect neural networks in your brain. Research has shown that the highly stressful nature of emotional abuse causes sensitive parts of the brain to be underdeveloped or reduced in volume.

The medial temporal lobe parts involved in learning, memory, and emotional expression are affected. The severity of the damage depends on the severity of the maltreatment. If toxic parents raised you, biological and psychological reasons are causing your challenges for various mental health conditions and general wellness."[xx]

4. Depression and Anxiety

"You're susceptible to poor mental health. Depression and anxiety are common occurrences in survivors of emotional manipulation. These adverse life situations cause us to develop negative ways of looking at the world. Our thoughts become biased and unrealistic, making us think of possible bad outcomes.

Are you usually worried about things that can go wrong? Do your thoughts generally make you feel negative feelings?

Since thoughts are a behavior, our thinking patterns can become habits. Specific ways of thinking are unhelpful as they deteriorate our mental health. They impact how we see ourselves, others, places, and situations. Depression and anxiety are thought disorders caused by such unhelpful thinking patterns."[xxi]

5. Substance Abuse

"You indulge in substance abuse.

Do you smoke, drink, or take drugs to cope with your difficulties? Is it hard for you to quit them despite facing adverse consequences?

Severe manipulation leaves people feeling isolated and numb. Studies have shown that the lack of social interaction leads to choices that form addictions. The high probably feels like a welcome change from the constant numbness.

Alternatively, substances also help suppress painful memories and feelings. The senses serve as a quick and familiar coping mechanism if you feel any resentment, anger, loneliness, or hopelessness. Sadly, addiction further deteriorates mental health and makes it harder for you to overcome your issues."[xxii]

Now that you know the negative health effects of manipulation, it is time to consider the moral implications of using manipulation in different situations.

Is Manipulation Morally Wrong?

Manipulation of individuals feels wrong when we are the victims of it, but can manipulation be a good thing? Noggle uses a few examples of when we might need to put aside our preconceptions of the morality of manipulation, and think about the situation more critically.

"Suppose that Tonya is a captured terrorist who has hidden a bomb in the city. Her preferred course of action is to keep its location secret until it explodes.

And suppose that Irving is an FBI interrogator who wants Tonya to reveal the bomb's location before it explodes. How would this way of filling in the details of the case change our moral assessment of the various ways that Irving might induce Tonya to change her mind?"[xxiii]

Noggle explores three possible answers, beginning with the most extreme and certain:

Yes, it is Wrong.

"One rather extreme answer would be: "not at all." This hardline view would hold that manipulation is always morally wrong, no matter the consequences. Since this hardline view resembles Kant's notorious hardline position that lying is always wrong, one might look to Kant's ethics for considerations to support it. But just as hardly anyone accepts Kant's hardline position against deception, the hardline view against manipulation also seems short on defenders."[xxiv]

Kant's idea that you should act in such a way that, if everyone acted in that manner, the world would continue to function is a basis for the moral idea against lying to manipulate people. This view is easy to hold when you are being lied to or manipulated, but Noggle urges us to consider other frames of looking at the problem.

To An Extent

"A less extreme position would be that while manipulation is always *pro tanto* (meaning to an extent) wrong, other moral considerations can sometimes outweigh the *pro tanto* wrongness of manipulation. Thus, we might think that manipulation is always harmful. Still, countervailing ethical factors might sometimes suffice to make manipulation justified on balance. What might such factors include? One obvious candidate would be consequences—for example, the fact that Irving's successful manipulation of Tonya would save many innocent lives. Non-consequentialist factors might also be countervailing considerations: Perhaps the immorality of Tonya's character, or the fact that she is acting on an evil desire or intention, is a countervailing factor that can outweigh the *pro tanto* wrongness of Irving's manipulation."[xxv]

In the preceding view, Noggle considers if Manipulation is immoral only to an extent and it can be outweighed by other issues. In the next view, Noggle considers whether manipulation might be good in certain circumstances.

Until Proven Otherwise

"By contrast, we might hold that manipulation is merely *prima facie* (meaning accepted as correct until proved otherwise) immoral. On this view, there is a presumption that manipulation is terrible, but this presumption can be defeated in some situations. When the idea *is* defeated, manipulation is not wrong (i.e., not even *pro tanto* wrong). On this view, we might say that while manipulation is usually inappropriate, it is not bad at all in the terrorist scenario."[xxvi]

Noggle does not rest on his exploration, but, rather, combines the preceding views to make a case for manipulation being wrong until it is proven less wrong than absolutely.

It's Complex

"A more complex—but, perhaps, ultimately more plausible—view would combine the *prima facie*, and *pro tanto* approaches. Such a view would hold that manipulation is *prima facie* immoral. Still, the wrongness is *pro tanto* rather than absolute when it is wrong. On this view, there are situations in which the presumption against manipulation is defeated, and manipulation is not even *pro tanto* wrong."[xxvii]

However Noggle spins it, Manipulation is at least sometimes wrong.

At Least Somewhat Wrong Some of the Time

"No matter how we answer whether manipulation, in general, is absolutely immoral, *prima facie* immoral, *pro tanto* immoral, or not even presumptively immoral, there are situations in which manipulation is terrible. Any complete answer to the evaluation question must explain why manipulation is awful in those cases where it is immoral. In addition, any view that holds that manipulation is only *pro tanto* and *prima facie* immoral should tell us what sorts of considerations can defeat the presumption that it is evil or outweigh its *pro tanto* immorality. Several accounts have been offered to identify the source of the moral wrongfulness of manipulation (when it is wrong)."[xxviii]

CONCLUSION

Our review of the literature on manipulation has concluded. If you or a loved one are in an abusive situation, please contact the National Domestic Violence Hotline at 8007997233 (USA). If you have realized that you need counseling, please reach out to a local qualified therapist or other mental health professional.

If you found this work informative or useful, please leave a positive review.

WORKS CITED

[i] Stritof, Sheri. "Is There Manipulation in Your Relationship?" Verywell Mind, March 1, 2022. https://www.verywellmind.com/manipulation-in-marriage-2302245.

[ii] Ibid.

[iii] Lehman, James, and Dee B. "Control Manipulative Child Behavior." Empowering Parents. Empowering Parents, February 2, 2021. http://web.archive.org/web/20220308181044/https://www.empoweringparents.com/article/masters-of-manipulation-how-kids-control-you-with-behavior/.

[iv] Ibid.

[v] Ibid.

[vi] Ibid.

[vii] Ibid.

[viii] Ibid.

[ix] Oliver, Ruby. "How to Cope with Manipulative Family Members." WeHaveKids. WeHaveKids, December 14, 2014. https://wehavekids.com/family-relationships/Musts-When-Coping-With-Scheming-Family-Membets.

[x] Shortsleeve, Cassie. "How to Tell If Someone Is Manipulating You-and What to Do." Time. Time, October 16, 2018. https://time.com/5411624/how-to-tell-if-being-manipulated/.

[xi] Ibid.

[xii] Ibid.

[xiii] Ambrozy, M., and Dominika Sokolovská. "(PDF) Media Manipulation in the Mass Society and the Role of Critical Thinking." ResearchGate. unknown, March 19, 2021. https://www.researchgate.net/publication/350176007_MEDIA_MANIPULATION_IN_THE_MASS_SOCIETY_AND_THE_ROLE_OF_CRITICAL_THINKING

[xiv] Ibid.

[xv] Timset, "Media Manipulation: 10 Strategies the Media Uses to Manipulate US." Exploring your mind, August 24, 2020. https://exploringyourmind.com/10-strategies-of-media-manipulation/.

[xvi] Ibid.

[xvii] "Manipulation." GoodTherapy.org Therapy Blog. GoodTherapy LLC, March 26, 2019. http://web.archive.org/web/20211220100946/https://www.good-therapy.org/blog/psychpedia/manipulation.

[xviii] Process., OptimistMindsLearn about our Editorial, and OptimistMinds. "5 Long-Term Effects of Manipulation." OptimistMinds. OptimistMinds, January 24, 2022. https://optimistminds.com/5-long-term-effects-of-manipulation/.

[xix] Ibid.

[xx] Ibid.

[xxi] Ibid.

[xxii] Ibid.

[xxiii] Robert Noggle, "The Ethics of Manipulation," Stanford Encyclopedia of Philosophy (Stanford University, March 22, 2020), https://plato.stanford.edu/entries/ethics-manipulation/.

[xxiv] Ibid.

[xxv] Ibid.

[xxvi] Ibid.

[xxvii] Ibid.

[xxviii] Ibid.

www.ingramcontent.com/pod-product-compliance
Lightning Source LLC
Chambersburg PA
CBHW060532280326
41933CB00014B/3143